I0487278

CREATING A SALES MENTALITY

Jarvis El-Amin

Dr. Omega AUNTIE Mothersill

VIVID VISION PUBLISHING

Creating A Sales Mentality

ISBN:978-1-4357-8543-4

First Printing: April 2022

Printed in the United States of America

Published by: Vivid Vision Publishing

Lakeland, Florida 33806

DEDICATION

Brother Ronald "Malik" Teart

Sunrise - *May 13, 1952* – *Sunset* - *August 14, 2021*

I met Brother Malik in the summer of 1977, at the Muslim take-out restaurant Arabian Fish & Steak. The restaurant was in the heart of Liberty City (Miami). I was fresh out of high school and new to Miami, from Dawson, Georgia. I was 17 years-old, sharp as a whip and the manager at the restaurant. My friendship with Malik grew quickly as we worked on several projects together, while attending the same Mosque. Brother Malik would frequent the restaurant often, giving him the opportunity to observe me in my work environment. He would often reference my people skills and mannerism. I can remember clearly the owners coming in and stating that upon the sale the new owners would bring in their own management and staff.

Hearing this sad news my spirits were low and you could see it on my face. Brother Malik saw my unhappy disposition and asked me what had made me so down. I told him what was going on and that I was about to lose my job! He listened as a great Mentor does, and then he told me not to worry! What I like about Brother Malik is that he did not just console me, he offered me a solution in the form of an opportunity! He stated that he would take me to a local wholesaler, where I could purchase merchandise to sell. This was the beginning of a beautiful relationship, with Malik as well as with sales. I not only value Malik as a friend but as the man who introduced me to the world of sales. We went from city to city, state to state and even door to door selling our wares. They shared many ups and downs in their 20+ years as sales brothers. I dedicated this book to the legacy of Brother Ronald "Malik" Teart affectionately known as "The National Spokesman for the rejected and downtrodden, as well as the "Mighty Malik" I happy to say we celebrated over 40 years of brotherhood and friendship.

May Allah forgive him for his sins and grant him access to paradise.

Jarvis El-Amin

DEDICATION

To the Delegates of the Women Business Leaders and Entrepreneur Pageant:

I dedicate this book to all Delegates pass, present and future. I know it takes courage, vision, dedication, and love to start, run and sustain a business. More importantly it takes SALES! You may not all sell a physical product, but you all must sell yourself, your ideas, and your brand to be successful in business. I learned from my sales mentor Brother Jarvis El-Amin to always be selling. Another great Sales Coach, Mary Kay Ash adapted from Thomas Watson Sr stated: nothing happens until someone sells something. Mary Kay Ash also taught her consultants it was "just as honorable to sell as it is to buy."

For many years I had a strong love/hate relationship with sales. I remember one day Brother Jarvis asked me to prepare a bag of my products. I was obedient and did what he asked. He picked me up, took me to a beauty salon, miles from my home and said I could not come out of the salon until I sold something. That was my first and only hard sell. I practically sold the entire bag and have been successfully selling ever since.

I believe in each of your visions, and I wish you grand success. I know that creating a pure sales mentality will not only change you, but it will also change your relationship with money. Selling is a powerful tool to combat poverty and lack. ABS (Always Be Selling). You will never lose in business if you continually apply the ABS method to your business.

Ladies of WBLEP keep Glowing and Growing... Success is yours!

Dr. Omega AUNTIE Mothersill your proud Director.

CONTENTS

CREATING A SALES MENTALITY

How Do You See Yourself
As A Salesperson

JARVIS K EL-AMIN &
DR. OMEGA 'AUNTIE' MOTHERSILL

DO YOU SEE YOURSELF AS A SALESPERSON?

JARVIS EL-AMIN and OMEGA AUNTIE MOTHERSILL

"Two great adages have influenced my sales career: 'It is just as honorable to sell as it is to buy,' and 'nothing happens until somebody sells something.' If one idea could capture the element that sets top performance apart, it would be customer focus. Outstanding sales depend on your ability to think from the customer's point of view and understand and respond to your customer's best interests. Successful salespeople know how to interpret what they hear their customers say. They not only listen, but they also hear what the customer really means."

Mary Kay Ash

INTRODUCTION

In a world where everyone likes everything in an instant! Where everything is fast paced and on the go! We all stop to think 'What's Next'! It will be up to you to sell yourself on what is coming next. I learned long ago to talk myself through it, to make every decision I make count. So, I tend to weigh the pros and cons of my decisions and pray the decision I make will pay out positively.

As the owner of seven pageants that celebrates women, men. and children. I must sell each Contestant on why they should try my program, for me to have stage participants for the live pageant every June. Yes, I must be excitingly convincing! Yes, I must provide enough information. Yes, I must know my product, my brand as well as my ideal client. This is all a part of the sales process.

Thanks to my sales mentor and coach, Bro. Jarvis El-Amin, I overcame my fear of selling. I am now a Master Seller and Closers. Those early years were rough. After several coaching sessions Bro. Jarvis identified that I had a poor understanding of sales. Thereby causing me to have a poor relationship with sales and selling. After a bit of tough intervention and a few intensive role-playing sessions, I was ready to give it a try.

My first independent sales experience was a jewel. I did as my mentor instructed. I put some products in a bag, and he

JARVIS EL-AMIN and OMEGA AUNTIE MOTHERSILL
dropped me off. When he came back to pick me up my bag
was nearly emptied. That was one of the most rewarding

experience I had ever had! Money in hand from cold calling, I was hooked! I did not stop booking appointments, however, on Saturday's cold calling became my new jam. I liked the instant revenue from sales.

Bro. Jarvis introducing me to sales helped to not only create a sales mentality but to define and streamline sales for me as well. This book was written to help open the entrepreneurial mind to the unlimited possibilities of sales. Sales for me started in the mind. In this book you will find many of the activities Bro. Jarvis introduced to me to help me in Creating A Sales Mentality.

<u>IDENTITY</u>

If you have no concept of who or what you are, achieving your goals in life will be uncertain. Without a well-defined identity, your ability to succeed will depend on chance and/or luck. Defining your identity will keep you focused as you set priorities, organize tasks, deal with emergencies, and accomplish challenges in your personal, family, professional and community endeavors.

If you have no concept of your identity, you run the risk of trying to be everything and do everything in a random, haphazard way.

In this session you will become aware of yourself and how to achieve your goal(s) by defining different elements of your self-image. You will assess your attitude, your habits, your likes, dislikes, as well as your abilities. Knowing yourself will allow you to make smart decisions about where to be, what to do, and with whom to associate. It will also allow for how to do what you need to do for you to be successful. You cannot believe in yourself until you KNOW yourself! Identity equals recognition. We can easily get caught up mirroring or mimicking others. The old saying

'Fake it… until you make it' has many of us emulating and coping others instead of discovering who we really are as a person, salesperson and/or entrepreneur. Knowing who you are is the key to success in business and career. I'm not saying, don't have someone you look up to and trust. I'm also not saying, don't have a mentor or someone whose advice you trust. What I am saying is not to lose yourself in other people's perceptions of who you are or should be.

Discover your identity as a person, salesperson, entrepreneur, or business leader in the upcoming exercises. See what you can learn about yourself by probing your mind and heart. Answer every question for the best possible results for self-understanding as well as self-awareness.

SELF-IMAGE
(One's conception or view of one's own abilities, identity, and worth)

Taking an honest look at yourself is not as easy as people try to make it seem. Really looking at yourself isn't easy. Some people prefer to imagine themselves in the future rather than looking at their present situation. Looking ahead plays a significant role as you set your goals and work toward them, but you must first make an honest assessment of where you are now. An honest assessment of oneself is needed to know where you are now before you can assess where you are going.

Many people have an extremely poor self-image. We are not saying you do, but how will you ever know unless you complete a true assessment. Take a minute to think about the people you know who seem to have a poor self-image of themselves. Observe how that hinders their ability to make the most of themselves and their lives. You will find that you do the same thing to yourself when your self-image doesn't match reality. Your goal is to define your self-image, so that it eventually reflects your true self, authenticating your self-image.

Assessing yourself honestly is crucial because

you create yourself through what you think of yourself. As a man thinketh, so is he!

What you think of yourself is what you bring about, wholeheartedly. A poor self-image can stagnate and paralyze you. The less you think you can do, the less you will try to do, and consequently the less you will achieve.

As you define yourself, avoid defining yourself in terms of:

External Things

It's easy to define yourself by external things such as: cars, neighborhoods, clothes, job titles, etc. But what happens to your identity if you lose these things? That is why it is important to focus on the things in your life that endures: the personal relationships that are important to you, the quality of your life, your professional ethics, and goals as well as your personal integrity. Define yourself in terms of elements that are fundamental to who you are and how you believe and behave.

Expectations

When we make decisions or behave because we feel we should, we might be letting other people's expectations determine our identity. Separate other's expectations from what you expect of yourself. Ultimately, you must be able to comfortably live with yourself. Constantly and consistently expect more of yourself. When you expect more from yourself, you produce more. Self-expectation is in direct correlation to personal success

Stereotypical Roles

It's sometimes easy to let roles determine how we act and see ourselves. But traditional, stereotypical roles such as "wife/mother/nurture," "husband/father/provider," "professional," "corporate executive" and "business owner" can limit our potential. Your various responsibilities are an important part of your self-image, but don't define yourself solely by them. You are more than a role or title. What you think about… you bring about!

WHO AM I?

List the 10 most important things that characterize YOU.

1. _____

2. _____

3. _____

4. _____

5. _____

6. _____

7. _____

8. _____

9. _____

10. _____

ATTITUDE

Your attitude affects everything you do. It can energize you or stop you, because it affects how you see yourself and the things you do. A positive attitude can open your mind to a learning experience, it will inspire you to take action, and help you to contribute to the welfare of others. On the other hand, a negative attitude can hinder learning, stifle initiative, and create stress for others.

What is your attitude about:

GOD

_____

_____

Family

_____

_____

Education

_____

_____

Civic/Community Duties

_____

_____

Finance

_____

_____

Social

_____

_____

The Future

_____

_____

Other

_____

_____

<u>LIKES AND DISLIKES</u>

In order for an individual to grow spiritually, mentally, financially, emotionally, and socially he/she must know their likes and dislikes. Knowing this about yourself will help determine your success at achieving your goals.

List five things you like about yourself

1. _____

   _____

2. _____

   _____

3. _____

   _____

4. _____

   _____

5. _____

   _____

List five things you most dislike about yourself

1. _____
   _____

2. _____
   _____

3. _____
   _____

4. _____
   _____

5. _____
   _____

Don't look at this as self-criticism, view it ss self-management. Only you can manage your shortcomings.

ABILITIES

As you think about what you like, your abilities will come to mind, because we often like best the things we can do well. Some abilities seem to be natural; you've learned to do some things without ever having to work too hard. Others you've struggled to develop and continue to work hard to maintain your level of expertise. Let's see what some of your abilities are:

1. What do you seem to be able to naturally do well?

   _____

   _____

   One word that describes you:

   _____

2. What have you worked hard on to be able to do?

   _____

   _____

   One word that describes you: _____

3. What do other people tell you are your natural abilities?

   _____

   _____

   One word that describes you: _____

4. What do other people praise you for doing well and
   working hard at?

   _____

One word that describes you: _____

5. Have your abilities changed over time?

   _____

One word that describes you: _____

<u>STRENGTH and WEAKNESSES</u>

For better directions on reaching your goals, there is a
need to know what your strengths and weaknesses are.

List Your Strengths:

1. _____

2. _____

3. _____

4. _____

5. _____

6. _____

7. _____

8. _____

9. _____

10. _____

STRENGTH and WEAKNESESS

Areas in which you are weak can offset your goals
Recognize your weaknesses and
List two ways you can improve them:

1. _____

2. _____

3. _____

4. _____

5. _____

6. _____

7. _____

8. _____

JARVIS EL-AMIN and OMEGA AUNTIE MOTHERSILL

1st Way I can improve:

_____

_____

2nd Way I can improve:

_____

_____

<u>SOME OF MY GREATEST</u> <u>ACCOMPLISHMENTS</u>

1. _____

2. _____

3. _____

4. _____

5. _____

6. _____

7. _____

8. _____

9. _____

10. _____

This list should be used as a motivational tool for whenever you are feeling down and or feeling as if you can't achieve something.

HABITS

(A recurrent, often unconscious pattern of behavior frequently acquired through repetition.)

Anything that you become accustomed to doing in a certain way, and often on a regular basis or at certain times, constitutes a habit. Your habits reveal a lot about you. So-called unpleasant habits earn that title because they can prevent you from reaching important goals. You have the power to change your habits. List five problematic habits you have and the effects of each one.

1. _____
   _____
   Effect: _____

2. _____
   _____
   Effect: _____

3. _____
   _____
   Effect: _____

CREATING A SALES MENTALITY

4._____

_____
Effect: _____

5._____

_____
Effect: _____

Out of the five, choose the habit you most want to change.

_____

_____

What helpful habit do you want to develop in its place?

_____

_____

One way to help yourself abandon your old habit is to think about how your new habit will improve your life. List three new habits and their benefits:

1. _____

Benefit: _____

2. _____

Benefit: _____

3. _____

Benefit: _____

Set yourself a deadline; give yourself three to four weeks to complete your habit shift. Keep track of your progress by indicating how well you did each week.

Week 1: _____

Week 2: _____

Week 3: _____

Week 4: _____

Don't forget to reward yourself for your hard work. Write here what your reward will be when you feel like you are on the road to a new and beneficial habit.

_____

_____

_____

_____

BUILDING PERSONAL WORTH

- Attitude: Have a positive attitude.

- STAR: Apply the STAR model (Situation, Task, Action, and Results)

- Value of Independence: Be self-reliant

- Ambition: This is a focus on your purpose.

- Drive: Commitment to action

- Sensitive to Peoples Problems: Extend a little grace to people.

- Articulation Skills: Record and listen to yourself speaking.

- Developing an Analytical Mind: Question first, answer last.

- Enjoy Solving Peoples' Problems: The art of entrepreneurship.

- Ethical: The right and wrong in your conduct.

- Sincerity: Freedom from hypocrisy

- Reliable Self Discipline: Being able to push yourself forward.

- Enthusiastic: The art of being excited or interested in something.

- Imagination: Forming innovative ideas and concepts.

- Initiative: Keep going when things get tough.

- Great Verbal Skills: The use of language to convey a point.

- Poise: Self-confidence & assurance tempered with knowledge

- Dress for Success: What you wear matters.

- Invest in your Image: You can't sell a dream looking like a nightmare.

<u>BENEFITS OF CREATIVE SELLING</u>

- Identity: Creating brand recognition.

- Self-image as a Salesperson: Your personal mental picture must be clear and positive.

- Nature & Significance of Selling: Being able to provide the consumer with the products or services that they want or need.

- Creative Selling: Creating alternate ideas to solve a consumer's problem.

- Salesperson as a:

    - Communicator: Convey and exchange information

    - Problem Solver: Solution oriented

    - Educator: Help consumers to acquire knowledge

    - Human Relations Expert: One who can handle conflict

- People Skills: Ability to interact with others

- Recognizing Buyers Behavior: Recognizing the consumers unmet needs.

- Understanding Body Language: Understanding the consumers' nonverbal signals.

JARVIS EL-AMIN and OMEGA AUNTIE MOTHERSILL

•

THE SUCCESSFUL SALES FORMULA

"After each presentation, summarize in your presentation that achieved positive results. Keep those and delete anything that did not achieve positive results. Only in this way can you polish your sales technique to ensure sales success. Remember, it is as honorable to sell as it is to buy. Practice will sharpen your skills and enhance your position as a professional salesperson. Salespeople are not born; they are made."

Mary Kay Ash

<u>SUCCESSFUL SALES FORMULA</u>

1. Need Analysis
   a. Understanding the customer's needs by probing with questions.

2. Need Awareness
   a. Making the customer aware of their needs.

3. Need Solution
   a. Lead with need
   b. WIFM (What's In It For Me)

4. Need Satisfaction
   AAFTO (Always Ask For The Order)
   a. Close the Sale

5. Getting Past the Gate Keeper
   a. Personal First Name
   b. Personal Financial Matter

6. Creating your "niche" in the Marketplace:

U. S. P.
(Unique Selling Proposition)

- U = Unique – What's unique or different about your product / service from your competitor to the benefit of your customer.

_____

_____

- S = Selling – Advantage, promotion, price, and customer service to the benefit of your customer.

_____

_____

- P = Proposition – Special offer, ethical inducement to take positive action.

_____

_____

Example: ADT Security has a $500 theft protection

<u>EMPATHY vs. SYMPATHY</u>

1. Understanding the customers' feelings

2. Show sincere interest in the customers' feelings

3. Not looking for a sympathy sale

4. Allow the customer to make an informed decision

PART I OF THE SUCCESSFUL SALES PROCESS: NEED ANALYSIS

1. The proper questions enable you to gain the prospect's trust.

2. To combine emotion and logic:
   a. Use "thinking" and "feeling" questions
   b. Use the three-question close
   c. Use a "talking pad" so the prospect can "see" the idea.

3. The successful sales professional is a word merchant and a picture painter.

4. Probe the prospect with three kinds of questions:

a. Open Door Questions
b. Closed Door Questions
c. Yes or No Questions

5. The least-developed tool of the professional salesperson is the VOICE. To develop this important tool:
   a. Practice, practice, and practice!
   b. Record your voice and your presentation.
   c. Drink warm water before speaking.
   d. Exaggerate opening your mouth.
   e. Smile.

COMBINING EMOTION AND LOGIC

Let's presume you have a product or service that saves your prospect money. At the end of your demonstration or presentation, when you have conclusively shown that your products or service does indeed save the prospect money, you should ask three questions:

- "Can you see where our product would save you money?"
- "Are you interested in saving money?"
- "If you were ever going to start saving money, when do you think would be the best time to start?"

One of the strongest emotions we face is FEAR. And you probably have heard the old sales adage, "Fear of loss is greater than the desire for gain." Obviously, you are trying to help the prospect by taking away the fear of losing money. (You didn't create the fear; you are helping eliminate it.) Your first question ("Can you see where our product would save you money?) begins the "fear elimination" process. You are now speaking to your prospect on an *emotional* level.

The second question may seem obvious, but it must be asked. This direct question ("Are you interested in saving money?") brings the prospect from the world of emotion into the world of *logic*. "Of course, I'm interested in saving money; a sensible person is interested in saving money" would be the mental response, even if the oral response is simply yes.

Now, by the prospect's own admission, your product saves money, and the person is adamant in the desire to save money. Question three ("If you were ever going to start saving money, when do you feel would be the best time to start?") calls for immediate action! It also is a reminder "emotionally" that failure to act might result in further losses of money.

OVERCOMING OBJECTIONS

"The successful sales professional asks the question to understand and identify the objection."
Zig Ziglar

<u>OVERCOMING OBJECTIONS</u>

Steps to overcoming objections:

Step 1 – Re-state the objections

Step 2 – Empathize with the customer

Step 3 – Re-state the benefits (WIIFM – What's In It For Me) or the results of your product/service

Step 4 – Isolate the objection by probing
Example: the only reason you wouldn't go ahead and get protected (benefit statement) is because of budget issues?

Step 5 – Assume the Sale

Step 6 – Stop talking (don't oversell or overkill your presentation)

OVERCOMING OBJECTIONS TECHNIQUE

Feel / Felt / Found Technique…

Example: I understand how you <u>feel</u> Diane, I've often <u>felt</u> the same way too, but what I've <u>found</u> is that you can….

JARVIS EL-AMIN and OMEGA AUNTIE MOTHERSILL

SUCCESSFUL CLOSING TECHNIQUES

A = Always
B = Be
C = Closing
The ABC's of Sales

Dr. P. Rhone Sanderson
Psychotherapist / Motivational Speaker

<u>SUCCESSFUL CLOSING TECHNIQUES</u>

- **Cost vs. Value:** The balance between the cost (price) of an item or service vs. the overall benefit

- **Assume the Sale:** A selling technique known as presumptive close. Where the salesperson intentionally assumes that the customer/client has already said yes to the sale.

- **Price vs. Cost:** The cost the company pays to produce a product vs. the actual cost the consumer pays for the product. Like wholesale vs. retail.

- **Need Satisfaction Close:** A sales approach where the salesperson probes into the needs of the consumer/customer/client.

Three Question Close:

Can you see?

_____
_____
_____

Are you interested in?

_____
_____
_____

When do you think?

_____
_____
_____

Example: *Tracey,* **can you see** *yourself walking on the WBLEP stage receiving your crown and sash in your business name?* **Are you interested in** *representing you as well as your business in a national pageant for women in business? Great, Tracey,* **when do you think** *you will be ready to complete your application and secure your title with an initial deposit?*

JARVIS EL-AMIN and OMEGA AUNTIE MOTHERSILL

SUGGESTED DIALOGUE

"Repetition is the mother of learning and the father of action, which makes it the architect of accomplishment."
Zig Ziglar

CALLING YOUR CUSTOMER/CLIENT

Some suggested dialogue you may want to use when calling your customer/client:

"Hello, may I please speak with (customer/client name)? (Customer's first name), this is (your name), (company name or your title). Do you have a few minutes?"

Once he/she says yes, immediately explain the purpose of the call:

"I was giving you a courtesy call for (your product/service). Okay! "Great." "I can come out to you, or you may drop by the office, which is better for you Tuesday or Friday? (Choice of two positives).

Confirm appointment or product order. Thank customer/client for time and/or order and disconnect the call.

CALLING CUSTOMERS FOR BIRTHDAY/ANNIVERSARY

"Hi, (customer/client name). This is (your name), (company name or your title). I just wanted to wish you happy birthday / happy anniversary today. (Offer any special promotion that you may have). If I can be of any assistant to you, your family, or your friends, please feel free to give me a call. Then terminate the call with enjoy your birthday."

SPECIAL MAILING

"Hi, (customer/client name). This is (your name), (company name or your title). Do you have a minute? I'm calling because I wanted to make sure that you received my letter/invitation/flier/brochure that I sent you. Did you receive it? Great! (re-state the promotion and terminate call).

JARVIS EL-AMIN and OMEGA AUNTIE MOTHERSILL

FOLLOW-UP AND FOLLOW THROUGH

"Persistence sells. Did you know that 50 percent of all salespeople give up when they fail to sell a customer on the first call? Only 25 percent make two calls and only 12 percent make three. Those who make three are the ones who succeed."
Mary Kay Ash

<u>FOLLOW-UP TIPS</u>

- Write thank you notes to client/customers
- Make notes to call new leads within two days
- Send birthday / anniversary cards
- Make courtesy calls
- Always have specific reason for call
  - Referral
  - Promotion

Keeping In Touch With Your Customers

Your customers are the lifeline of your business, so be sure to follow up with them. Treat them as if each one of them is wearing a sign that says, "Make me feel important." Following up with customers is one of the ways you can do this!

Customer Service Phone Calls or Text

You'll want to allot some time each week for making your customer service calls via phone or text. A half-hour each day devoted to customer service calls can provide you with an important and consistent avenue of income.

Why It Is Important To Follow Up

Following up with your customers/clients shows them how much you care. They may even change their thoughts about you and your business. Customers/Clients just want an authentic and respectful experience and will go elsewhere if they are not getting it from your business or company.

GOAL SETTING

"The longer I live, the more deeply I'm convinced that the difference between the successful person and the failure, between the strong and weak, is a decision."
Willie E. Gary, Attorney

DEFINITION OF GOAL

A **Goal** is an objective, aim and/or purpose

A **Goal** is a dream, an idea being acted upon

THE IMPORTANCE OF GOALS

Goals provide direction for your life.

Goals focus your activities

Goals will provide you with internal control to make things happen the way you want them to.

Goals help you prioritize the areas and activities that concern you.

Goals lead to balance and a perspective to the use of your resources.

"Without **Goals** individuals just wander through life, they stumble along never knowing where they are going so, they never get anywhere."

GOAL SETTING

In order to get somewhere, you must know three things:

1. Where you are going?

2. How you expect to get there.

3. When you will arrive.

OBJECTIVES

At the end of this session, you should be able to:

- Understand the goal setting approach and the reason it's effective.

- Apply the goal setting approach to both your personal and professional life.

- Reduce goals to manageable size.

- Write a goal statement in measurable terms.

- Translate a goal into action.

W's and a H of GOAL SETTING

WHO   Every goal represents a personal commitment to achieve! You must accept the responsibility of that commitment while, at the same time, involving others if you want them to be committed to the goal.

WHAT   Goals are statements of measurable results you want to Achieve. They translate your wishes into reality and give you a basis to decide where you should concentrate your efforts.

WHEN   Goals must be tied to a specific period. You must decide when something is to begin and when it is to be completed in order to measure your success.

WHERE A person during a lifetime will have many opportunities to set and achieve many goals, knowingly or unknowingly. Wherever you are in your lifespan, if you are not goal oriented, it's easy to get started. Start where you are.

WHY   Goals can only be accomplished when they are selected, defined, and translated into actions. To get somewhere you need to know:

1. Where are you going?
2. How do you expect to get there?
3. When should you arrive?

WHICH To determine your goals, you need to select your priorities, what you want most and expect out of life. You must decide which goals are important for you to work on!

HOW   A goal is established by determining an area of concern or special interest within which you want a specific result.

FOCUS ON GOALS

Find below a few basic tips on goals from Dr. Omega AUNTIE Mothersill:

Why Set Goals?

1. When goals are set, big things start to happen.
2. Achieving goals makes you feel good about yourself.
3. Goals will provide attitude checkup.
4. Setting goals establishes self-discipline and motivation.
5. Having goals gives you direction and purpose.
6. Goals take you to desired results.
7. Goals will create good habits and proven patterns.
8. Setting goals will eliminate others from controlling and pulling on your life.

Set daily, weekly, monthly, and yearly goals to discipline yourself. If you don't, others will.

Goals Can Be Negative If:

1. They are too big with no planned purpose.
2. They are out of your sphere and scope of interest.

3. You believe it will take luck and not perseverance to achieve the goal.
4. If you compare your weaknesses to other people's strengths.
5. You develop and set your goal by comparing yourself with others' accomplishments.
6. You are setting the goal for someone else.

Never set a goal because of someone else's thoughts or belief. People always think they know what's best for you, however, it's important that you know what's best for you! SET YOUR GOALS!

Reasons Most People Do Not Set Goals:

1. They are not sold on or believe the goal to be beneficial.
2. They feel it's outside of their comfort zone.
3. They fear feeling overwhelmed at making such a commitment.
4. The fear of failure or success.
5. They have a poor vision, purpose, attitude and/or focus.
6. They don't want to put in the work.

Setting A Goal

1. Know exactly what you want and be specific.
2. PUSH yourself… a big goal should never feel comfortable. Stretch yourself to the limit.
3. Create mental images. The subconscious mind accepts all fed and given information as factual. It cannot distinguish between what is real and what is imagined or believed.
4. Involve those who believe in you. (i.e.: family members) What can they expect if you achieve your goals?
5. Find you a rabbit (someone you can model). Preferably someone in your industry that's doing amazing things.

6. Define who and where you are in life, career, or business. Goals should be "sizable" according to your talents and abilities.
7. Determine how to break a goal down to span a day, a week, a month, and a year.
8. Write your goals in detail and talk about them with interested people that you trust to hold you accountable.
9. Work towards your daily goals. If a goal is not worked on for three consecutive days, it's as if it never existed.
10. Visualize goals as if they have already happened.
11. Keep your FOCUS (Follow Once Course Until Successful) on your Goals.
12. Quitting is NEVER an option.
13. Once you have achieved a goal set another one immediately.

GUIDELINES FOR EFFECTIVE GOAL SETTING

1. Get clear on the idea of who, what, when, where, why, and how you want to achieve your goals in life.

2. Effective goals are written down.

    a. You must write down your goals, it is the first step toward achieving them.
    b. Committing your goals to paper allows them to become concrete.
    c. For your goals to be effective, they must be written in specific and measurable terms.

3. Your goals should be measurable so that your progress can be evaluated, adjusted, and ultimately achieved.

4. Effective goals can be visualized to be realized.

    a. Picture yourself in heart and mind reaching your goals.
    b. Visualize your results, the moment, and the feeling you will experience when you reach your goal.

5. Effective goals are achievable.
   a. Goals need to challenge your skills and abilities, without discouraging your effort and performance.
6. Goals need a timeframe.
   a. Give yourself enough time to complete your goals.
   b. In an event the original date set for the goal is not reached, don't change the goal, change the date.
   c. Make sure the timeframe set is reasonable and obtainable.
7. Effective goals are divided into smaller units, when this is done, it becomes easier to manage and complete your goals.
   a. Break your goals down into bitesize pieces.
   b. Don't make them so small that they become irrelevant.
   c. Celebrate all your wins/completions, even the smaller ones. This keeps you motivated and encouraged.

8. Effective goals are analyzed for their potential pitfalls and problems.
   a. As you establish your goals, consider the steps you will take to accomplish your goals.
   b. Critical thinking while analyzing your goals will help you to cover all angles allowing you to stay on the winning path toward achieving goals.
9. Effective goals require action. This helps to eliminate or minimize the consequences of potential pitfalls or problems.
   a. Actionable is your buzz word. Make sure you are daily work towards your goal. If you fail to plan, you plan to fail. Work on your goal!
10. Effective goals must be viewed regularly to maintain and ensure
    progression of goals.
    a. Review your goals daily in the morning before you start your day to readjust your goals accordingly. Some like to review their goals at the end of the workday to streamline a plan of action for the next workday.

    b. Periodic review of your goals will help to ensure they continue to be realistic, timely and relevant.

11. Effective goals yield results and rewards that are valuable to you.

    a. You must stay motivated to work toward your goals. It pushes you to get through the process.

    b. As you establish each goal, identify at least one meaningful reward you would like to give yourself!

    c. Celebrate your successes.

REACHING YOUR GOALS

1. Understand and know what you want.

2. Demand of yourself clear, precise answers to these questions:

   a. What do I want to accomplish with my life?

   b. What do I want to be in life? and

   c. What does it take to satisfy me?

3. Identify the benefits of reaching your goal.

4. Know the tools and resources required for reaching your goal.

5. Work with goals that are relatable and compatible.

6. Concentrating on those things that relate to your goals.

7. Be diligent and persistent.

8. Be willing to ask for help, make it a team effort.

9. Look at things not as they are, but as they can be.

   Visualization adds value and truth to everything. (A big thinker always visualizes what can be done in the future; he/she isn't stuck in the present).

10. Review your progress toward your goals on a regular basis.

My ten most Important goals are: *(Choose goals that are compatible)*

1. _____

2. _____

3. _____

4. _____

5. _____

6. _____

7. _____

8. _____

9. _____

10. _____

This list will help to provide direction for your life and help you focus your daily activities for maximum results.

My _____ year(s) goals for:

Personal Development:

_____
_____
_____
_____
_____

Family:

_____
_____
_____
_____
_____

Financial:

_____
_____
_____
_____
_____

Education:

_____
_____
_____
_____
_____

JARVIS EL-AMIN and OMEGA AUNTIE MOTHERSILL

Community:

_____
_____
_____
_____
_____

Professional:

_____
_____
_____
_____
_____

Health:

_____
_____
_____
_____
_____

<u>YOUR LIFETIME GOALS</u>

1. What are your lifetime goals (think bucket list)?

_____

_____

_____

_____

2. How would you like to spend the next five years?

(Be specific):

_____

_____

_____

_____

3. If you knew you only had 12 months to live, how would you spend it?

_____

_____

_____

_____

_____

_____

<u>HOW TO SET GOALS</u>

1. Create a commitment agreement and sign it:

_____
_____
_____
_____
_____
_____

2. Tailor your goals to a manageable size:

_____
_____
_____
_____
_____
_____

3. Make goals measurable and add a completion date:

_____
_____
_____
_____
_____
_____

4. Initiate an action plan (daily, weekly, monthly, and yearly):

_____

_____

_____

_____

_____

_____

BUSINESS TOOLS

JARVIS EL-AMIN and OMEGA AUNTIE MOTHERSILL

"Opportunity does not send letters of introduction."
Naomi Sims
Model and Entrepreneur

<u>BUSINESS TOOLS</u>

- Goal Posters
  - Make your goal poster. You can start with a piece of paper or poster board.
  - Glue or tape pictures of your goals on your poster, as well as pictures of the people you want to benefit from achieving these goals.
  - Have fun and be creative.
  - You can use magazines, brochures, and pictures to complete your poster.

- Focus Folder (F.O.C.U.S.) Follow Ones Course Until Successful…
  - This is what we call your accomplishment folder.
    - Testimonials
    - Flyers or posters of events you participated in or created
    - Awards and rewards
    - Recommendation letters
    - Compliments and praises

- Scheduling System App or Calendar
  - Here are a few great scheduling apps:
    - Acuity Scheduling
    - Schedulicity
    - Calendly
    - Booksy Biz
    - Microsoft Bookings
    - Zoho
    - Setmore
    - Doodle
    - YouCanBookMe

  - Calendar for scheduling internal and external appointments
    - Appointments
    - Client Meetings
    - Interviews
    - Zoom Meetings
    - Personal Appointments
    - Holidays and
    - Birthdays

- Journal or Notebook
- A wonderful place to write down daily notes. The good, the bad and the ugly. I call this the... what can I do better than I did yesterday list.
- 3 Most important things to do list Appointments
- Affirmations
- Notes from reading material
- That a girl/boy (Celebrations)

- Digital Business Card
- This for me is the best thing since sliced bread. COVID19 had everyone on edge. With a DBC you can store and share your contact information. No need to worry about space like you do for a traditional business card. You can store as much information as you want.
  - You can store your brand logo, link website, contact information, valuable resources, social media accounts and professional photos.
    - HiHello
    - Switchit
    - About.me
    - CamCard
    - KADO Network

- Power Jacket or Tie
    - This is always a confidence booster. I know for me it's a win/win feeling when I put on my Power Jacket. Men for you, it could be your favorite tie.
    - Find something in your wardrobe that makes you feel like a $million$ books and use it to win!

- Social Media Sites
    - In business or personal matters, it is great to have some form of social media pages. Social media is a proven an effective way to reach new clients. People buy from those they trust. Social media engagement can help a business or brand create and build trust. Below you will find some of the most used as well as the most profitable social media platforms being used in business today.
        - Facebook
        - Instagram
        - LinkedIn

- TikTok
- Google My Business
- YouTube
- WhatsApp
- Facebook Messenger
- WeChat
- Telegram
- Pinterest
- Reddit
- Twitter
- SnapChat
- Medium

- Payment Apps
  - Payment Apps are another useful tool. Payment Apps cater to every and all kinds of customers. In store or on the go Payment Apps allow business owners to make and take payments directly from and to a smart device. Payment Apps help to avoid the traditional payroll methods. You can connect a credit card, debit card or your bank account to a payment app. Most payment apps make transferring money simple and easy.
    - Google Pay
    - Apple Pay
    - Samsung Pay
    - PayPal
    - Xoom
    - Circle Pay
    - Square Cash (Cash App)
    - Zelle
    - Facebook Messenger
    - Venmo

Vending events may require you to accept credit cards. Here are a few recommended credit card processing services.

- Clover
- Payment Cloud
- Square
- LMS
- ProMerchant
- STAX

- Social Media Post Scheduler
  - We have already discovered how vital social media is to the working salesperson. Customers have an expectation that any companies or profession they are interested in would have some form of social media presence. Stay current and relevant on social media using a Post Scheduler.
  - Hootsuite
  - Lolly
  - Sandibel
  - Content Cal
  - Monday.com
  - Sprout Social
  - Everypost
  - Crowdfire

<u>WHAT YOU THINK ABOUT, YOU BRING ABOUT</u>

You must continue to "feed" your subconscious mind with positive information about your excellent work and success. You can do this through affirmation and visualization.

- Why is affirming important to your success?
  _____
  _____
  _____

- The affirmation card I will use daily for the next 30 days will say:
  _____
  _____
  _____

- How many times a day can you commit to affirming? _____

- How will you use visualization to help you achieve success?
  _____
  _____
  _____

It is a great idea to create an additional Affirmation Success Card that you are going to use and tape it on your mirror at home or someplace you will see it multiple times a day. Repeat your affirmation 3 times each day for 30 days straight.

MONEY MANAGEMENT

Record Keeping

- Maintaining accurate, up-to-date records will help keep your business organized, and could help you save money on income taxes.

- Maintaining accurate records will ensure that you can take advantage of all tax deductions or credits that you are eligible for on your income tax return.

- The IRS (Internal Revenue Service) expects taxpayers to have supporting documents for income and expenses that they report on a federal tax return. In the event of an audit, you must prove income and expenses with this supporting documentation.

- If documents do not effectively prove what is reported on the tax return, the IRS can determine that you owe more tax and penalty fees for the unpaid portion of the tax.

Using Envelopes

- Use two large envelopes (11'x14" or larger): one to store monthly business income information, and the other to store monthly business expense information.

- On the outside of one envelope, keep a running tab of mileage and expenses. In the other list any income produced.

- Insert the appropriate information throughout the month and file the corresponding paperwork month. At the end of the month, add up columns on both envelopes. The totals should give a benchmark of income and expenses and help with budgeting for the following month.

- The two envelopes should be completed like this every month of the year. At the end of the year, there should be a total of 24 envelopes.

- The 24 completed envelopes are used by you or your accountant or tax advisor at the end of the year to prepare your business tax return.

- Store Income Statements and stubs that show proof of income inside the envelope and record the corresponding information on the front of the envelope.

- Insert in the envelope any sales receipts and bank deposit slips. Record the corresponding information on the front of folder.

- Always retain a receipt for business expenditures; then note the item purchased, as well as whether you paid by cash, check or charge.

- Keep a record of cash expenditures with no receipt (such as business phone call from a public telephone or a toll charge) as they occur.

- Enclose your monthly bank statement from your business account and your monthly Master Card or Visa Statement.

- Include receipts or canceled checks for any business-related expenses, for example, postage, and office supplies.

SUPPLIES CHECKLIST

You can purchase supplies at a local office supply store, drug store, etc. The following are suggested supplies to set up an efficient office.

- Write It Down
  - Wall calendar and/or desk calendar
  - Datebook
  - Notepaper
  - Notebook paper
  - Pens and pencils
  - Correction tape

- File It
  - Address Book or Rolodex (for keeping track of your customers' addresses and telephone numbers)
  - Notebook (for storing copies of contracts or agreements)
  - Organizer (for birthday, anniversary, get well, baby cards, etc.)
  - Hanging file folders
  - Accordion file folders (two or three)

- Keep It Together
  - Stapler and staples
  - Paper clips
  - Rubber bands
  - Scotch tape
  - Packing tape
  - Glue stick
  - Desk Organizer
  - Things to do
  - Paper weight

- Mail It
  - Stamps (USPS Online)
  - Business envelopes (letter and legal size)
  - Large manila envelopes
  - Bubble-Light shipping bags
  - Bubble wrap
  - Packing Tape
  - Thank You Cards
  - Letterhead (Stationary)
  - UPS Account
  - Fed-Ex Account
  - DHL Account (International Mailings)
  - PO Box (If you work from home)

- Miscellaneous
  - Pencil Sharpener
  - Scissors
  - Money Bag
  - Dictionary
  - Hole Punch
  - Calculator
  - Laptop
  - Sanitizer
  - Tissue
  - Wipes
  - Desktop
  - iPad
  - Desktop Tripod
  - Ring Light
  - Photo Box

<u>ORGANIZE YOUR WORKSPACE</u>

INSTRUCTIONS: Think *of exactly how you will design your workspace. Describe that space below. Review the Office Organization and Supplies Checklist and write down what supplies and files you will need and how you will organize your workspace.*

- My Office Area Visualized

  _____
  _____
  _____
  _____
  _____
  _____

- What I Need to Set Up My Workspace

  _____
  _____
  _____
  _____
  _____
  _____

- How to Organize My Workspace
- _____
  _____
  _____
  _____
  _____
  _____

INSPIRATIONAL

JARVIS EL-AMIN and OMEGA AUNTIE MOTHERSILL

"If there is no struggle, there is no progress."
Frederick Douglass
Abolitionist

<u>BELIEVE IN YOURSELF</u>

By: Norman Vincent Peale
www.nightingale.com

Believe in yourself! Have faith in your abilities! Without a humble but reasonable confidence in your own powers you cannot be successful or happy. But with sound self-confidence you can succeed. A sense of inferiority and inadequacy interferes with the attainment of your hopes, but self-confidence leads to self-realization and successful achievement. Because of the importance of this mental attitude, this book will help you believe in yourself and release your inner powers.

It is appalling to realize the number of pathetic people who are hampered and made miserable by the malady popularly called the inferiority complex. But you need not suffer from this trouble. When proper steps are taken, it can be overcome. You can develop creative faith in yourself-faith that is justified.

After speaking to a convention of businesspeople in a city auditorium, I was on the stage greeting people when a man approached me and with peculiar intensity of manner asked, "May I talk with you about a matter of desperate importance to me?"

I asked him to remain until the others had gone, then we went backstage and sat down. "I'm in this town to handle the most important business deal of my life," he explained. "If I succeed, it means everything to me. If I fail, I'm done for."

I suggested that he relax a little, that nothing was quite that final. If he succeeded, that was fine. If he didn't, well, tomorrow would be another day. "I have a terrible disbelief in myself," he said dejectedly. "I have no confidence. I just don't believe I can put it over. I am very discouraged and depressed. In fact," he lamented, "I'm about sunk. Here I am, forty years old. Why is it that all my life I have been tormented by inferiority feelings, by lack of confidence, by self-doubt? I listened to your speech tonight in which you talked about the power of positive thinking, and I want to ask how I can get some faith in myself."

"There are two steps to take," I replied. "First, it is important to discover why you have these feelings of no power. That requires analysis and will take time. We must approach the maladies of our emotional life as a physician probe to find something wrong physically.

This cannot be done immediately, certainly not in our brief interview tonight, and it may require treatment to reach a permanent solution. But to pull you through this immediate problem I shall give you a formula which will work if you use it."

"As you walk down to the street tonight, I suggest that you repeat certain words which I shall give you. Say them over several times after you get into bed. When you awaken tomorrow, repeat them three times before arising. On the way to your important appointment tell them three additional times. Do this with an attitude of faith and you will receive sufficient strength and ability to deal with this problem. Later, if you wish, we can go into an analysis of your basic problem, but whatever we produce following that study, the formula which I am now giving to you can be a large factor in the eventual cure. "Following is the affirmation which I gave him –

"I can do all things through Christ which strengthened me." (Philippians 4:13)

SUCCESS/FAILURE

By: Jim Rohn

Success is not to be pursued; it is to be attracted to the person you become.

Failure is not a single, cataclysmic event. You do not fail overnight. Instead, failure is a few errors in judgment, repeated every day.

Do not take the casual approach to life. Casualness leads to casualties.

It is too bad; failures do not give seminars. Wouldn't that be valuable? If you meet a guy who has messed up his life for forty years, you have just got to say, "John, if I bring my journal and promise to take good notes, would you spend a day with me?"

Success is not so much what we have as it is what we are.

Success is 20% skills and 80% strategy. You might know how to read, but more importantly, what's your plan to read?

Average people look for ways of getting away with it; successful people look for ways of getting on with it.

Seven Self-Motivators
By: Brain Tracy
(Excerpted from Brian Tracy's Success Mastery Academy)

Here are seven Self-Motivator reminders for you to review on a regular basis:

#1. Get Serious. You must decide to go all the way to the top. Up to now you have thought about it. Up to now, it has passed through your mind. Many of you have made the decision, and you have made up your mind to go all the way to the top, and your lives have taken off. It is the most extraordinary thing. Your life is one way, like in the shadow going up the dark side of the hill, until the moment you decide, "By gum, I am going to be the best at what I do. I am going to be in the top 10 percent." And suddenly you roll into the sunshine, and your life is forever different – wonderful. Get serious. Do not fool around anymore.

#2. Identify Your Limiting Step to Sales Success. What's your limiting step? What's the one skill area that's holding you back? What's the skill? What's the quality? What's the action? Ask other people. Find out what you need to become good at. Sometimes it may be only one skill.

If you became good on the telephone, you could double prospecting effectiveness and in turn double your sales. If you became incredibly good at getting the order at the end from qualified prospects, you could double your sales. If you became exceptionally good at managing your time, I mean to really manage your time well, you may be able to double your face time and double your income. Find out what is holding you back. What is the critical limiting step that is determining your success today?

#3. Get Around the Right People. Who are the right people? The right people are the people in this room. Get around winners. Get around positive people. Get around people with goals and plans, people who are going somewhere with their lives and have high aspirations. Get around eagles. As Zig says, "You can't scratch with turkeys if you want to fly with the eagles." And get away from negative people. Get away from toxic people that complain, whine, and moan all the time. Who needs them? Life is too short.

#4. Take Excellent Care of Your Health. Take excellent care of your physical health. That means a good diet, good exercise.

Everybody knows they should eat better foods, get regular exercise and especially lots of rest.

That's very important. If you're going to work hard 5 days a week, go to bed early 5 days a week. Get a good night's sleep. Be fully rested, and tonight get really rested. You don't have to watch the Letterman Show…

#5. Positive Visualization. See yourself as the best in your field. Remember, all improvement in your life begins with an improvement in your mental picture. Visualize yourself; see yourself as the best continually. You are the best. Isn't that, right? So therefore, see yourself as the best.

#6. Positive Self-Talk. Talk to yourself positively all the time. Control your inner dialogue. And what do you say to yourself? Say, "I'm the best." Say it. Say I'm the best. I like myself. I can do it. I love my work. Yes, that's how you talk to yourself. And the more you say it to yourself…someone may say, "Well, what if you say those things to yourself and you don't believe them. Isn't that lying to yourself?" No, that's not lying to yourself. It's telling the truth in advance.

JARVIS EL-AMIN and OMEGA AUNTIE MOTHERSILL

Because it doesn't matter where you're coming from –all that matters is where you're going. Talk to yourself the way you want to be, not the way you just happen to be at this moment. Remember, you may have gotten where you are today largely by accident. But where you're going in the future is purely by design.

#7. Positive Action. Get going. Move fast. Develop a sense of urgency. A sense of urgency is the one thing that you can develop that will separate you from everyone else in your field. Develop a bias for action. When you get a clever idea, do it now. Only 2% of people in our society have a bias for action. And if you're already in the top 10% you can move yourself to the top 2% by resolving that whenever you have an idea or something, do it now. And the faster you move, the better you get. And the better you get, the more you like yourself. And the more you like yourself, the higher your self-esteem is. And the higher your self-esteem is, the greater your self-discipline. And the more you persist; then you ultimately become unstoppable.

"Showing a profit means touching something and leaving it better than you found it." Jim Rohn

READING STRENGTHENS YOUR BRAIN

JARVIS EL-AMIN and OMEGA AUNTIE MOTHERSILL

*"Reading is the gateway skill that makes all other
learning possible"*
Barack Obama
44th President of the United States

TOP 40 SUGGESTED READING LIST

1. Look At Me NOW!
Dr. Omega AUNTIE Mothersill

2. Think and Grow Rich
Napoleon Hill

3. Maximize The Moment God's Action Plan For Your Life
Dr. T. D. Jakes

4. The Magic of Thinking Big
David Schwartz

5. Over the Top
Zig Ziglar

6. Mary Kay on People Management
Mary Kay Ash

7. What Makes the Great, Great
Dr. Dennis Kimbro

8. Live Your Dreams
Les Brown

9. /Feel the Fear and Do It Anyway
Susan Jeffers

10. You Deserve the Best
Pat Pearson

11. Zig on Selling

JARVIS EL-AMIN and OMEGA AUNTIE MOTHERSILL
Zig Ziglar

12. The Barefoot Executive
Carrie Wilkerson

13. I Bring Me, Confidentially
Dr. Omega AUNTIE Mothersill

14. You Can Become the Person You Want To Be
Dr. Robert Schuller

15. The Aladdin Factor
Jack Canfield

16. You Can Have It All
Mary Kay Ash

17. Virtuous Leadership
Alexander Harvard

18. The Power of Positive Thinking
Norman Vincent Peale

19. How To Win Friends And Influence People
Dale Carnegie

20. The Entrepreneur Mind
Kevin D. Johnson

21. The Richest Man In Babylon
George Samuel Clason

22. Successful Women Think Differently
Valorie Burton

23. The Great Investment: Faith, Family and Finance
Dr. T. D. Jakes

24. Dare To Lead
Brene Brown

25. Make Yourself Unforgettable
Dale Carnegie

26. The 7 Habits Of Highly Effective People
Stephen Covey

27. Think and Grow Rich: A Black Choice
Dr. Dennis Kimbro

28. Outliers: The Story Of Success
Malcolm Gladwell

29. The Confidence Code
Katty Kay and Claire Shipman

30. The Secret To Success
Eric Thomas

Reading 30 minutes a day can be done with minimal effort, and it can have a positive impact on your mental, emotional, and financial health!

SUCCESS BREEDS CONFIDENCE

"Confidence is as old as time and as young as your next thought of yourself!'

Dr. Omega AUNTIE Mothersill

Entrepreneur, Author & International Speaker

DO YOU NEED MORE, WANT MORE and WILLING TO DO THE WORK?

5 Common Characteristics Of Successful People:

1. They have Vision

2. They have a PLAN to achieve their visions and dreams

3. They have fine-tuned SKILLS and they cultivate their ABILITIES

4. They are willing to WORK HARD to achieve their Dream

5. They DON'T allow the NO's to STOP them

Which one resonates with you the most? #_____

5 Ways To Build Your Confidence:

1. Learn to acknowledge as well as accept compliments

2. Know your worth and promote its value

3. Self-doubt and self-criticism MUST be eliminated

4. Affirm your worth positively every day

5. Hang around people that celebrate you and your accomplishments

Which one resonates with you the most? #_____

5 Qualities Of An Effective Leader:

1. They work to develop others

2. They are strategic thinkers, innovators, and action takers

3. They invest in their own personal development

4. They operate integrally and ethically

5. They are effective communicators

Which one resonates with you the most? #_____

5 Traits That Makes The Great, Great!

1. They are great at cutting their losses and move on

2. They are great at delegating

3. They are great at persuasion and very charismatic

4. They are great at implementing and executing their vision

5. They are great at connecting to the right resources

Which one resonates with you the most? #_____

<u>CREATE A GREAT DAY!</u>

Today is a blank canvas upon which you can create a masterpiece. It's not just a chunk of time to be endured. It is an opportunity to live, to experience, to learn, to build, to grow and to make a difference. Today is full of ways in which you can move forward. To look at this day with the goal of "just getting by" is an enormous waste of the possibilities which are open to you at this very moment.

Right now, you're in a special place, a place filled with opportunity and promise. There's something you'll be able to do today that you've never been able to do today before, and you may never be able to do again. Make the most of that opportunity. Fulfill that promise. Take advantage of the exceptional circumstances while they're here.

How many times have you wished that you had the world at your feet, that you had the opportunity of a lifetime? Stop wishing. It's here. It's called today. The world is indeed at your feet. So go where you've been meaning to go. Do what you've been intending to do. Now is your grand opportunity. Get busy creating the unique masterpiece of today.

Ralph Marston

JARVIS EL-AMIN and OMEGA AUNTIE MOTHERSILL

<u>ACKNOWLEDGMENTS</u>

Thank you kindly for supporting me through the years. Be it mentoring, family, friends, classmates, buddies, business partners, community, political, events, etc... I am humbled and grateful. To those that pre-ordered Creating A Sales Mentality, your support means the world to me, thank you! Bro. Jarvis El-Amin

Josnet Scott-El-Amin
The Late Jimmie Bell My Mother
The Late Charlie C. Jones (Father)
The Late Otis Redding (Cousin)
(The Late) Yusuf "Ali" El-Amin (Mentor & Brother)
Claxton Williams (My Childhood Friend)
Dr. Omega AUNTIE Mothersill
Dr. Peggy & Landlin Earle
Terry O. Young
(The Late) Dr. Khallid Muhammad (Friend & Mentor)
Yvette Lewis
Shakira Racine
Tia-Skyy Scott-Hall
Aaliyah El-Amin
Saeed El-Amin
Saima Siddiqui
Nadiyah El-Amin
(The Late) Imam Qasim Ahmed (Spiritual Advisor)

Mayor Robert Albritten (First Mentor)
Michael Jenkins
Masjid An-Nasr
Abdul-Baqee (Mentor)
Marlon & Janel Brown
Keith Duhart
Sharon Johnson
Dr. Deonne Wilson
Chakirah Parker
Liz York-Cohen
Richard Muhammad
The Late Karim Ali (My Mentor, My Captain)
Rodney Jones
Imam Rasheed Abdullah
Starr Linette Brookins
Robin Lockett
Hiba Rahim
Imam Abdul Q. Aziz
Charlene Armor
Candy Lowe
Curtis and Selena Ward
Imam Tawheed Sams
Marvin Farr
Nadiyah Ahmad

Michael Muhammad
Principal Delia Gadson
Jackie Hearns
Eileen Jamison
Larry Scott
Scott Bigley
Renee Brown
Julia Jackson
Connie Melton
Kathy Hair
Diedrea Baldwin
Lance Smith
James Sanders
Jerone Young
Joshua Washington
Kathy Henry
Barbara James
Dawud El-Amin
Gerald Abdul-Wasi
Deana Schupp
Audley Lyte
Denise Pate
Janelle Mc Gregor

Keith Ware
Leo Walthaw
Rodney Hutchinson
Michael Mitchell
Hassan El-Shabazz
John Jenkins
Daryll DJ Jones
Mona Judge
Idris Muhammad
Hakeem Hameed
Libby Herring
Charles Kimbrough
Davina Ward
Cecelia Mitchell
Derrie " Dean " Rushdan
Terrance Ramses
Merrie Allen
Denise Pate
Sis. Connie "Marcus Garvey" Burton
Wanda Mundy
Imam Qasim Ahmed (Spiritual Advisor)
Harold Ford
Warren Thomas
Larry Muhammad

Harrison Ross
Bishop Michelle B. Patty
Corey "King Cobra" Felton
Daryl Johnson
Earline Terrell
Naheem Muhammad
Sister Izzy Boyd
Alfred Green
Shani Tobie
Kenny Rushing
Stacia Castellow
Spencer Pittman
Ricky Turner
Alfred Green

Patricia Cruse
Asiyah Rashid- Crow
Deborah McCray Grier
Gwen Tobie
Barbara Marshall (My Favorite Teacher)
Gregory Tobie "Jammin Greg Allen"
WTMP Howard Word
Florida Sentinel
Rev. Willie " Baby Gray" Dixon
Jacqueline Hinds
Sheereen Aarif
Benjamin Hollis

JARVIS EL-AMIN and OMEGA AUNTIE MOTHERSILL

<u>MEET THE AUTHOR</u>

Jarvis K. El-Amin was born to Charlie and Jimmie Bell Jones in Dawson, Georgia, October 18, 1959. Jimmie Bell is the second Cousin to Soul Legend "Otis Redding." Mr. El-Amin is an entrepreneur, author, community organizer and marketing consultant. Formerly an Account Executive for AM1150 WTMP. Jarvis sold over 4,000 copies of his book "From South Georgia to South Africa: The Journey on a Rocky Road to Success". He is an advocate for Economic and Political Empowerment. He has been involved in Voter Registration and Voter Education for many years.

JARVIS EL-AMIN and OMEGA AUNTIE MOTHERSILL
Mr. El-Amin has volunteered for many organizations in our community. He is a Founding Board Member for Masjid An-Nasr. He is Founding Board Member Emage-USA a Muslim Civic Education Organization, Founding Board Member for the Tampa Bay Muslim Alliance that sponsor the Annual Charity Festival, Member of the Executive Committee of the Local NAACP, President, and Co-Founder Regional Black Chamber of Commerce. Founding Board Member for Tampa Chapter of CAIR, Founding Member of Candy Lowe Conversation & Tea a Social Discussion Group and a former Board member of WMNF 88.5 Community Radio.

Mr. El-Amin is proud to be a practicing Muslim and a Caring Father and Grandfather. He enjoys socializing and networking.

OTHER BOOKS BY THE AUTHOR

- From South Georgia to South Africa

JARVIS EL-AMIN and OMEGA AUNTIE MOTHERSILL
<u>ACKNOWLEDGMENTS</u>

With my whole heart, I would like to thank my mom and dad for their continued love and support. I promise I have the best parents ever. To my siblings, family, and friends I love each of you to the moon and back. To MY pageant queens, I love you all individually as well as collectively. You ladies ROCK! To my students past and present, you guys keep me Glowing and Growing! To my clients and mentees what a pleasure and a joy it is for me to be your coach. This one is for each of you. You guys truly make my soul smile. Thank you.

To the ladies of REIGN, the Princess Program Pageant, and the Prince Program Pageant. You guys keep me young and on my toes. Thank you for trusting me to pour into your life. I love each of you beyond measure. To the International Women in Business and Leadership, I am coming for you! Look out WORLD Women Business and Entrepreneur Pageant in Going International in 2023.

To Cohort 2 of the National Entrepreneur Association and Dr. Zalonya Allen you guys helped me to push this book out. This bootcamp was everything I needed in a time such as this. What a fantastic opportunity and eye-opening experience. I pray each of you continue to soar! Last but certainly not least, thank you Heavenly Father, for being my Lord and my God. I move and have my being because of Who You are. Thank you for the many opportunities and blessings you have afforded me. I will continue to lean on and to trust you for I know all good things come from you!

Dr. Omega AUNTIE Mothersill

<u>MEET THE AUTHOR</u>

Dr. Omega 'AUNTIE' Mothersill is a champion of women, author, speaker, educator, success, model, pageant, and image coach who has served women all over the United States and abroad. She is the owner and executive director of Women Business Leaders and Entrepreneur Pageant and several other entities. She prides herself on helping women reach their full potential in life and business. Her burning desire is to see every woman living a whole, successful, confident, and productive life.

Omega believes in training children with the knowledge that they can go anywhere and do anything their heart desires. Knowing this is the key to ultimate success for girls around the world. She does this through the REIGN Organization (Regally Empowered Inspired Girls Network) and the Princess Program Pageant. Both are empowerment programs for girls. She coaches and serves girls ages 3 – 18.

Her personal motto to live by… God choose what we go through, we choose how we go through it! REIGN in your confidence!

<u>OTHER BOOK BY THE AUTHOR</u>

- Persist To Pursue in Live Fanatical: 13 Stories of Trailblazers Who Are Living Bold, Inspired Lives! By Bridgett Washington (Book Compilation).
- I BRING ME, CONFIDENTLY!
- Look At Me Now!
- WBLEP Women In Business Calendar 5th Edition

<u>Coming in 2022</u>

- My Little Pageant Black Book (eBook)
- 90 Days to a More Positive, Powerful and Productive Me! - (eBook)
- 28 Ways To Boost Your Confidence

<u>Coming in 2023</u>

- My Crown Ain't Plastic – 13 Awesome Pageant Queens share Pageantry, Purpose, and Platforms. (Book Compilation)
- I Am My Fathers Daughter (The Absenteeism Of My Biological Father and The Ever Presence of My Heavenly Father)

JARVIS EL-AMIN and OMEGA AUNTIE MOTHERSILL

www.ingramcontent.com/pod-product-compliance
Lightning Source LLC
Chambersburg PA
CBHW051532170526
45165CB00002B/704